Toronto

RAPTORS

BY JIM GIGLIOTTI

Published by The Child's World®
1980 Lookout Drive • Mankato, MN 56003-1705
800-599-READ • www.childsworld.com

Cover: © Jonathan Hayward/Canadian Press/AP Images.
Interior Photographs ©: AP Images: Michael Dwyer 6; Ron Froehm 6;
Franklin Gunn/Toronto Star 17, 26; Bill Kostrom 18. Newscom: Icon SW 5,
26; Christine Chew/UPI 12, 21; Gary Green/MCT 22; Chris Williams/Icon
SW 25; Jerome Moore/Icon SW 26; Leah Klafczynski/TNS.
Imagn/USA Today Sports: Dan Hamilton 10; Nick Turchiaro 26.
Shutterstock: JHVEPhoto 13.

ISBN 9781503824492
LCCN 2018964292

Printed in the United States of America
PA02416

ABOUT THE AUTHOR

Jim Gigliotti has worked for the University
of Southern California's athletic department,
the Los Angeles Dodgers, and the National
Football League. He is now an author who
has written more than 100 books, mostly
for young readers, on a variety of topics.

TABLE OF CONTENTS

GO, RAPTORS!

The Raptors are one of the newest teams in the NBA. In 2019, they won their first NBA championship. The Raptors are the first team from Canada to do that. They have fans from coast to coast in that country. The Raptors played hard to become the champs. Can they do it again? Let's find out more about this up-and-coming team.

NBA All-Star Kawhi Leonard joined Toronto in 2018 and led the Raptors to the championship.

Fred VanVleet is a key player off the bench for Toronto. Here, he battles Atlantic Division rival Boston.

WHO ARE THE RAPTORS?

The Raptors play in the Atlantic Division. That division is part of the NBA's Eastern Conference. The other teams in the Atlantic Division are the Boston Celtics, the Brooklyn Nets, the New York Knicks, and the Philadelphia 76ers. The Raptors have won the Atlantic Division five times. In 2018–19, they made the **playoffs** for the sixth year in a row.

WHERE THEY CAME FROM

The Raptors are the only NBA team based in Canada. They began play in the 1996 season. They were an NBA **expansion team**. The club's owners let the fans vote for a team name. The winner was Raptors, a type of dinosaur. Raptors were famous from the movie *Jurassic Park*. Plus, many dinosaur **fossils** have been found in Canada.

Toronto had the No. 2 pick in the 1996 NBA Draft and took Marcus Camby. He shows the Raptors old dinosaur logo to NBA Commissioner David Stern.

Long and lean, Pascal Siakam was a key scorer for Toronto in 2019.

WHO THEY PLAY

The Raptors play 82 games each season. They play 41 games at home and 41 on the road. They play four games against each of the other Atlantic Division teams. They play 36 games against other Eastern Conference teams. Finally, the Raptors play each of the teams in the Western Conference twice. That's a lot of basketball! In June, the winners of the Western and Eastern Conferences play each other in the NBA Finals.

WHERE THEY PLAY

At first, the Raptors played their home games at the Toronto SkyDome. It was huge! The SkyDome was so big it included a hotel, a fitness club, and a theater. The team moved to the new Scotiabank Arena in 2000. The Toronto Maple Leafs hockey team also plays there. Raptors fans gather outside the arena in an area called "Jurassic Park."

Scotiabank Arena

WELCOME TO
Scotiabank Arena

This arena in Toronto is home to basketball and hockey. During NBA games, Raptor the mascot (left) has fun!

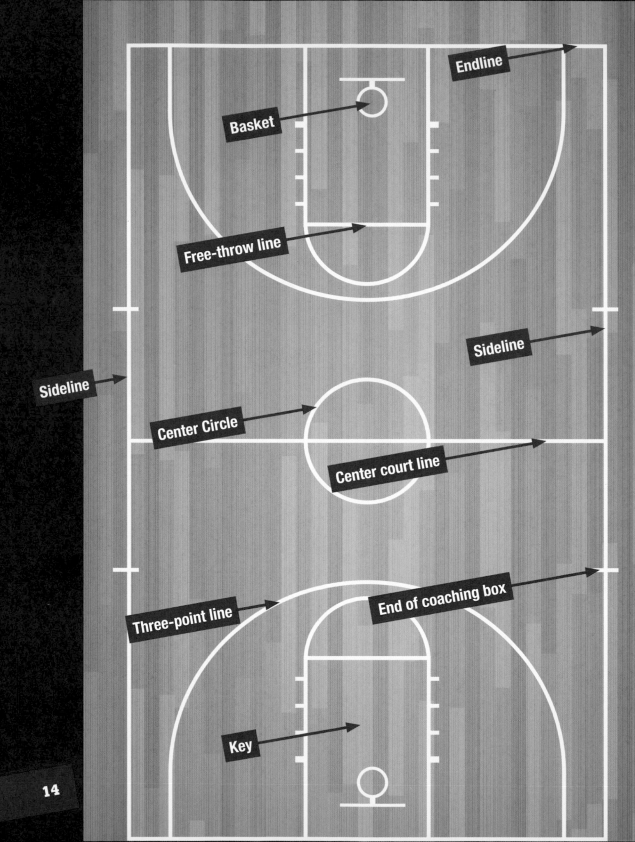

Endline

Basket

Free-throw line

Sideline

Sideline

Center Circle

Center court line

Three-point line

End of coaching box

Key

THE BASKETBALL COURT

An NBA court is 94 feet long and 50 feet wide (28.6 m by 15.24 m). Nearly all the courts are made from hard maple wood. Rubber mats under the wood help make the floor springy. Each team paints the court with its logo and colors. Lines on the court show the players where to take shots. The diagram on the left shows the important parts of the NBA court.

Scotiabank Arena is photographed on Instagram more than any other place in Canada.

GOOD TIMES

In 2019, the Raptors thrilled all of Canada by winning the NBA championship. Toronto beat the Golden State Warriors in seven games. Kawhi Leonard was named the NBA Finals MVP. Another Raptors highlight came in 2018. DeMar DeRozan scored 52 points in a game against the Milwaukee Bucks. That was the most ever by a Raptors player.

17

Kawhi Leonard shows off the 2019 NBA championship trophy.

Losing was nothing new for Toronto in 2009. Losing to former Raptors star Vince Carter was tougher, though.

TOUGH TIMES

Most expansion teams have a few rough seasons. The worst came in 1998 for the Raptors. The team won only 16 games. The team missed the playoffs five years in a row starting in 2009. The Raptors led the Nets by 18 points in a game that season. The Nets came back to win. The winning points were scored by Vince Carter. He used to be the Raptors star. That hurt!

ALL THE RIGHT MOVES

Vince Carter is known for two amazing dunks. One was a reverse 360 to win the NBA Slam Dunk Contest in 2000. Another came in the Olympics that year. He soared over a 7-foot 2-inch (2.18-m) opponent from France. Carter slammed the ball home! Current star Kawhi Leonard's best moves are on defense. His quick hands make him a top ball stealer.

The NBA Slam Dunk Contest is held every year on the weekend of the NBA All-Star Game.

Chris Bosh (4) was an All-Star in five of his seven seasons with Toronto.

Vince Carter was the NBA **Rookie** of the Year in 1999. He was the Raptors' first all-star the next season. DeMar DeRozan holds many team records. He played the most games in team history. He scored the most points, too. Chris Bosh grabbed the most rebounds. Antonio Davis was an all-star center. In 2001, he helped the Raptors win a playoff series for the first time.

HEROES NOW

Point guard Kyle Lowry is a star player. **Forward** Kawhi Leonard is, too. The Raptors made big trades to bring them to Toronto. Forward Pascal Siakam was a surprise star in 2019. Guard Fred VanVleet hit key shots in the playoffs. When the team needs a big lineup, it turns to Marc Gasol. He stands 7 feet 1 inch (2.15 m) and was born in Spain.

Kyle Lowry drives to the hoop for a layup. Lowry is the key to the Raptors' offensive success.

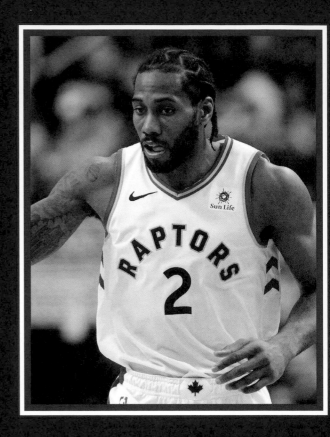

WHAT THEY WEAR

NBA players wear a **tank top** jersey. Players wear team shorts. Each player can choose his own sneakers. Some players also wear knee pads or wrist guards.

Each NBA team has more than one jersey style. The pictures at left show some of the Raptors' jerseys.

The NBA basketball is 29.5 inches (75 cm) around. It is covered with leather. The leather has small bumps called pebbles.

The pebbles on a basketball help players grip it.

H ere are some of the all-time career records for the Toronto Raptors. These stats are complete through all of the 2018–19 NBA regular season.

ASSISTS PER GAME

Damon Stoudamire	8.8
T.J. Ford	7.2

POINTS PER GAME

Vince Carter	23.4
Chris Bosh	20.2

STEALS PER GAME

Doug Christie	2.1
Kyle Lowry	1.5

REBOUNDS PER GAME

Chris Bosh	9.4
Antonio Davis	9.2

THREE-POINT FIELD GOALS

Kyle Lowry	1,223
Morris Peterson	801

FREE-THROW PCT.

Jose Calderon	.877
Lou Williams	.861

GAMES	
DeMar DeRozan	675
Morris Peterson	542

DeMAR DeROZAN

GLOSSARY

expansion team *(ek-SPAN-shun TEEM)* a new team that starts from scratch

forward *(FORE-word)* a player in basketball who usually plays away from the basket

fossils *(FAH-suhls)* parts of an organism that have been preserved in the earth's crust

Hall of Fame *(HALL UV FAYM)* a building in Springfield, Massachusetts, that honors basketball heroes

playoffs *(PLAY-offs)* games played between top teams to determine who moves ahead

point guard *(POYNT GARD)* a basketball player who most often dribbles and passes the ball

rookie *(ROOK-ee)* a player in his first season

tank top *(TANK TOP)* a style of shirt that has straps over the shoulders and no sleeves

FIND OUT MORE

IN THE LIBRARY

Big Book of Who: Basketball (Sports Illustrated Kids Big Books). New York, NY: Sports Illustrated Kids, 2015.

Doeden, Matt. *The NBA Playoffs: In Pursuit of Basketball Glory.* Minneapolis, MN: Millbrook Press, 2019.

Whiting, Jim. *The NBA: A History of Hoops: Toronto Raptors.* Mankato, MN: Creative Paperbacks, 2017.

ON THE WEB

Visit our website for links about the Toronto Raptors:
childsworld.com/links

Note to Parents, Teachers, and Librarians: We routinely verify our Web links to make sure they are safe and active sites. So encourage your readers to check them out!

INDEX